PAY OFF YOUR MORTGAGE IN 3 YEARS:

The 4-Step System That Will Save You Years and Thousands in Interest Payments

ERIC BLANKENSTEIN

*Dedicated to my life guiding lights –
Jonathan and Maya*

How to Pay Off Your Mortgage in as Fast as Three Years: the Four-Step System That Will Save You Years and Thousands in Interest Payments

© 2019 Eric Blankenstein

All rights reserved. No part of this publication may be reproduced, distributed, or transmitted in any form or by any means, including photocopy, recording, or other electronic or mechanical methods without the prior written permission of the publisher.

While all attempts have been made to verify the information provided in this publication, neither the author nor the publisher assumes any responsibility for errors, omissions, or contrary interpretation on the subject matter herein. This book is for entertainment purposes only. The views expressed are those of the author alone and should not be taken as expert instructions or suggestions. Examples in this book are presented for educational purposes only. The reader is responsible for his or her own actions.

Neither the author nor the publisher assumes any responsibility or liability whatsoever on behalf of the purchaser or reader of this book. Any perceived slight of any individual or organization is purely unintentional.

Bonus

Download the free mortgage amortization spreadsheet from www.financial-wisdon.net.

CONTENTS

Introduction 1

Chapter 1 - The Components Of A Mortgage 7
The Mortgage Components 8
Mortgage Products In The Us 14
Three Government-Backed Mortgage Types 16
Timely Advice If You Have Not Bought A House Yet 18

Chapter 2 - Why You Should Pay Off Your Mortgage Debt Fast 20
Definition Of A Mortgage 20
Us Mortgage Statistics 21
Why You Should Pay Off Your Mortgage As Quickly As You Can? 22
    What Happens On A 30-Year Amortization Loan ... 22
    What Happens On A 15-Year Amortization 25
What Does It Mean? 28
Points To Remember 28

Chapter 3 - How To Pay Off Your Mortgage In A Few Short Years 31
The Concept 33
Here Is How The Four-Step System Will Work 36
In Case You Don't Have Enough Equity In The House
.... 44
A Few Caveats To Remember: 54
Some Tips To Help You Set This In Motion: 56

Chapter 4 - How To Accelerate Your Mortgage Payment With Other Options 58

Set Up Biweekly Payments 59

Add An Extra Sum Each Month 61

Cut The Amortization On Your Loan 63

Use Your Tax Refund To Pay Down Your Principal ... 64

Put Your Raise To Work 66

Chapter 5 - How To Pay Your Mortgage In As Little As Three Years 68

Phase 1: Heloc/Ploc 1 70

Phase 2: Heloc/Ploc 2 71

Phase 3: Additional Monthly Payments 72

A Few Caveats To Remember 73

Chapter 6 - How Remarkably Different Will Be Your Financial Situation If You Pay Your Mortgage Faster
.... 76

The Smiths Versus The Joneses 77

Here Is What Happens As Time Progresses 79

A Few Caveats To Remember 82

Chapter 7 - My Speedy Mortgage Payoff Story 84

Chapter 8 - Conclusion 92

I Challenge You To Be Different 94

What Are The Next Steps? 95

References 96

INTRODUCTION

A man in debt is so far a slave.
Ralph Waldo Emerson

Do you have a mortgage? Is the cost of carrying your mortgage a heavy burden on your finances? If your answer is yes, you are not alone. You picked the right book to read because in this book I will show you exactly what to do to eliminate your mortgage debt quickly and without changing your lifestyle or payment amount. If you are willing and/or capable to do more, this book will take you to the extreme and will show you how you can pay off your mortgage debt in as quickly as three years.

Here are some eye-popping facts:

The average originated loan amount in the US is $243,761.[1]

Mortgage debt is the largest form of debt among American consumers. The total value of outstanding mortgage debt in the United States according to the US Federal Reserve Bank amounts to 15.13 trillion US dollars (that is a *trillion*) as of the end of second quarter in 2018.[2] This is absolutely a staggering amount of debt, and someone is making money from lending it. Can you guess who?

Well, I will tell you. In 2017,

- Banks originate 43.9 percent of mortgages.[2,3]
- No depository lenders originate 47.1 percent of mortgages.[2,3]
- Credit unions originate about 9 percent of mortgages.[2,3]

Are you part of this statistic?

If you are, you are not alone. This book will open your eyes to how mortgages work and why it is in your best interest to pay off your mortgage as soon as possible.

In Canada, our neighbor to the north, the situation is similar.

- Banks hold 74.2 percent of mortgages.[4]
- Credit unions hold 12.5 percent of mortgages.[4]
- Life insurance companies hold about 3.8 percent of mortgages.[4]
- The balance is held between pension funds, non-depository institutions, and mortgage loan companies.[4]

The numbers are somewhat smaller, but they paint a very similar picture as the US market.

Who Is This Book For

This book is definitely for you if you have a mortgage. If you have a mortgage on your home, recreational property, investment property, or any other property for that matter, this book can *change* your life. I know it sounds grandiose and pretentious, but I promise you once you read this book, it will open your eyes to understand how expensive is mortgage debt, the possibilities to reduce it, and how exactly to structure your finances to eliminate this beast of a home mortgage, which probably represents the biggest debt most of us face in our lifetime.

This book is also valuable to anyone contemplating buying a home in the near or far future. It will open your eyes and make you aware as to what to look for and how to structure your mortgage debt from the outset.

In addition, with the purchase of this book, I will provide you with a link to our *free* mortgage calculation spreadsheet, which is an Excel spreadsheet that will help you visualize and comprehend where your money goes when you take a mortgage. It will help you in a more numerical way to see where you are now with your mortgage, how your money is going (what portion goes to pay interest and what portion goes to reduce your debt), and how to implement the suggestions in this book to pay off your mortgage in the fastest way possible based on your own finances and particular situation. Remember, individual circumstances, income, and financial positions are different. That is why by loading my free Excel spreadsheet and crunching your own particular numbers, your own financial picture will become clearer, and you will gain an insight specific to your own particular situation.

My Promise to You

I promise that your road to better finances can start here if you have focus, determination, and are willing to put in some work. What you're about to read in this book is simple, down-to-earth, tested advice that can work for many people. It worked for me (see my story on Chapter 7), so it will work for you as well, as long as you take action once you understand the concept.

This book will give you the inside look into the mechanics behind a mortgage, one of the most daunting debt instrument and how it is designed to take hostage the borrower for many years to come. We will outline different techniques one can use to break free from a traditional mortgage paying process and how most people will be able to implement this process within a span of two to three months.

My four-step process will show you what exact step to take and how to implement them. Once you set this plan in motion, you will see the benefits quickly enough to make you commit to it and pay off your mortgage debt in a few short years. If you are capable financially and prepared to take a more aggressive approach, Chapter 5 will show you the way to pay your mortgage in as *quickly* as three years.

If anything, in the worst-case scenario, this book will open your eyes to understand the mechanics behind most mortgage product, and it will show you different ways to pay off your mortgage years sooner, therefore saving you a substantial amount of money.

When you are done reading this book, you will understand where your mortgage payment is going, how *expensive* mortgages are, and the four-step strategy to pay off your mortgage years earlier. If the four-stage system does not work for you, there is also mention of other steps you can take to pay your mortgage years faster.

It begins here with reading this book through, understanding the concepts, and then applying them to your own situation. As the years go by, you pay off your mortgage years earlier and use the money that's been freed up to build your wealth (see Chapter 6).

Can you imagine the freedom of not paying a mortgage? What would it do to your life? Can you imagine the freedom? Can you see the possibilities?

I am sure you can, and I am sure if you have a mortgage, you want to break the 30-year shackles and be mortgage free in a few short years.

Is it doable?

Absolutely it is. I have done it, and so can you. However, it takes some work to set up this process, and it takes persistence to stay the course and not deviate. The immense rewards, as you will discover, outweigh the difficulties. It will open your life to a new world and many opportunities to build wealth and financial security.

Obviously, results may vary depending on your particular circumstances. However, with this book, you will get the outline of how to do it and also different options to as to how to pay your mortgage faster. The actual implementation of my four-step system will be up to you. The longer you wait, the worse it gets. Abraham Lincoln reflected this notion in what he said in 1856: "***Action speak louder than words.***"

Are you ready? Let's get going! The first step is to keep reading.

CHAPTER 1 - THE COMPONENTS OF A MORTGAGE

Debt is like any other trap: easy enough to get into but hard enough to get out of.
Henry Wheeler Shaw

To make sense of your mortgage, it is important to first review and understand the different workings of a mortgage.

THE MORTGAGE COMPONENTS

There are five basic components of a mortgage:

- principal
- interest
- amortization
- taxes and insurance
- equity

Principal

This is the amount you initially borrow. It is the amount of money you ask the lender to give you to purchase the property you want to buy. With each payment you make to the lender, a portion is dedicated to repayment of the principal amount you owe. Let's look at an example. Say you are purchasing a house worth $350,000. Your down payment is 20 percent or $70,000, which leaves a balance of $280,000. When you borrow the $280,000 from a financial institution or any other lender to purchase the property, your initial principal amount is $280,000. It is reduced with each payment you make. However, in the first few years, only a small portion of the mortgage payments is allocated to reduce or repay the principal.

Interest

Interest is the amount of money you pay your lender for the right to borrow the principal amount. In other words, it is the lender's reward for lending you the principal amount. It represents the *cost of borrowing money*.

There are two types of interest loans: simple interest and compounded interest.

In simple interest, the amount of interest one pays or earns in the second period is not affected by the interest in the previous period. Simple interest is calculated by multiplying the *principal* by the *interest rate* by the *number of payment periods* over the life of the loan. It's a linear progression.

With a compounded interest, the amount of interest one pays or earns is calculated each period on the *original principal* and *all interest accumulated during past periods*. It is an exponential progression. In a compound interest loan, the unpaid interest at the end of the first period is added to the principal for the second period, allowing the interest to compound. You can think of compound interest as a series of back-to-back simple interest pacts. The interest earned in each period is added to the principal of the previous period to become the principal for the next period.

If you are into math and formulas, here is a fun website that explains how to calculate each mortgage and the required formulas.

https://www.mathsisfun.com/money/interest.html

Amortization

Amortization is a fancy word to describe the amount of time a loan or a mortgage will be paid off. It refers to the process of paying off a debt, usually a loan or mortgage, over a time period through paying a series of payments. A portion of each of these payments is allocated to interest, and a portion is allocated to pay off the principal balance of the loan. The portion of interest and the portion allocated to payment of the principal amount are determined in the loan amortization schedule. Initially, a large portion of each payment is allocated to interest and a small portion to repayment of the principal balance. However, as the loan progresses, larger portions of the payments are allocated toward paying down the principal. It takes many years for the portion of interest and principal payment to be about equal. For example, on a $200,000 loan at 5 percent amortized over 30 years, it will take 16 years and two months. This means in the first 16 years of this loan, the borrower pays *more* for interest than for principal repayments. That also explains why to borrow $100 costs almost $200 in total payments at the end of 30 years.

Taxes

Real estate taxes are a charge by the municipality/city or the governing authority of the jurisdiction in which the property is located. It is calculated or determined by a local government body based on the assessed value of the property and is paid by the owner of the property every year. The local governing body will use the assessed taxes to fund water and sewer improvements, schools, law enforcement, fire service, and other required and necessary services. Taxes are calculated by the governing authority on a yearly basis. However, the property owner can pay these taxes on a monthly, quarterly, or semi-annually, and most likely than not, they will be collected by your lender as part of your monthly payments.

The annual amount due is divided by the total number of monthly mortgage payments in a given year. In many cases, the lender collects the payments and holds them in escrow until the taxes have to be paid.

Insurance

Property insurance is a policy that provides financial protection and reimbursement to the owner of a property in the event of damage caused by fire, theft, or some other disasters. Property insurance can include homeowner's insurance, flood insurance, and earthquake insurance to mention few inclusions.

PITI is an acronym that stands for principal, interest, taxes, and insurance. While principal, interest, taxes, and insurance make up the *typical* mortgage payments, some people opt for mortgages that do not include taxes or insurance as part of the monthly payment. With this type of loan, you have a lower monthly payment, but you must pay the taxes and insurance on your own.

To determine an owner's monthly taxes and insurance portion if the lending institution collects the tax and insurance portion, the annual tax and insurance figures are added and then divided by 12 and are collected monthly with each payment.

Many lending institutions require the borrower to pay a monthly portion to pay the taxes and insurance. They require borrowers to do that to ascertain that the taxes and insurance are paid. Taxes take priority over the mortgage that is the reason so many lending institutions insist on collecting the tax money with each payment to make sure that the government taxes are fully paid. The same holds for insurance. Many lenders collect insurance as part of the monthly payment to make sure the insurance payments are made and the property is insured.

Equity

Home equity is the market value of a homeowner's unencumbered interest in their real property.[5]

To word it simply, it's the difference between the property's market value and the outstanding balance of all loans on the property. For example, if we have a property with a market value of $350,000 and we have a mortgage against the property with a balance of $222,000, the equity on the property is $128,000. (350,000 - 222,000 = 128,000).

Simple enough.

A more elaborate situation is if we have a property with a market value of $350,000, we have a mortgage against the property with a balance of $222,000. Let's say we have a HELOC (home equity line of credit) of $45,000. Then the equity on the property is 83,000 (350,000 - 222,000 - 45,000 = 83,000).

We will discuss HELOC later in the book in much more detail.

Let's talk a bit on the types of mortgages you see in the US market.

MORTGAGE PRODUCTS IN THE US

At the time of writing in late 2018, there are several types of loans available in the US market.

Fixed-rate mortgage loans, as the name suggests, have a fixed or the same interest rate for the duration of the loan. This means that your monthly payment will stay the same, month after month and year after year. It will never change. This is true even for long-term financing options such as the 30-year fixed-rate loan. It has the same interest rate and the same monthly payment for the entire term. A common reason many people choose fixed-rate mortgage loans is because it's predictable and the payment never changes for the duration of the loan, so they know each and every month what the mortgage payment will be.

Adjustable-rate mortgage loans (ARMs) are loans that have an interest rate that will change or adjust from time to time based on some criteria the lender chooses. Typically, the rate on an ARM will change every year after an initial period of remaining fixed. It is therefore referred to as a hybrid product. A hybrid ARM loan is one that starts off with a fixed or unchanging interest rate before switching over to an adjustable rate. For instance, the 5/1 ARM loan is an adjustable-rate mortgage with a 30-year term that is fixed for the first five years and adjustable for the remaining 25 years. This loan can adjust once each year after the first five years.

The first number is the fixed rate period, whereas 5 refers to the amount of years with a fixed rate. The second number is the rate at which the interest rate increases, 1 being once every year. The 5/1 ARM is just one type of adjustable rate mortgage. There are many other terms available in the market.

An ARM is best suited for buyers who plan on staying in the home for less than five years or who plan on paying off the loan in five years or less.

The 30-year fixed-rate mortgage is the most popular mortgage in America. However, that doesn't mean it's the right one for every person. Still, many homeowners would rather deal with the stability of a fixed-rate mortgage over the fluctuating payments of an ARM.

Mortgage Points

Mortgage points are in essence fees that the lender *may* charge the borrower if the borrower has poor credit or in markets where lending is very tight and restricted. One point is equal to 1 percent of the mortgage value. Therefore, on a $200,000 mortgage, one point would equal to $2,000 ($200,000 x 1% or $200,000 x 0.01 = $2,000).

There are other choices when it comes to type of mortgages as well. You'll also have to decide whether you want to use a government-insured home loan (such as FHA or VA) or a conventional type of loan.

A conventional home loan is one that is not insured or guaranteed by the federal government in any way. This distinguishes it from the three government-backed mortgage types explained below (FHA, VA, and USDA).

THREE GOVERNMENT-BACKED MORTGAGE TYPES

FHA Loan

FHA loans help make home ownership possible for borrowers who don't have the traditional 20 percent down payment and don't have pristine credit. Borrowers need a certain minimum FICO score (580 at the time of writing) to get FHA's maximum 3.5 percent financing. However, some lower credit score (500 at the time of writing) are accepted with at least 10 percent down. FHA loans require two mortgage insurance premiums: one is paid up front, and the other is paid annually for the life of the loan if you put less than 10 percent down.

VA Loan

VA loans provide flexible, low-interest mortgages for active-duty members and veterans of the US military and their families. VA loans do not require a down payment or PMI, and closing costs are generally capped and may be paid by the seller. A funding fee is charged on VA loans as a percentage of the loan amount to help offset the program's cost to taxpayers. This fee, as well as other closing costs, can be rolled into most VA loans or paid up front at closing.

USDA Loan

USDA loans help low-income borrowers buy homes in rural areas. The borrower must purchase a home in a USDA-eligible area and meet certain income limits to qualify. Some USDA loans do not require a down payment for eligible borrowers with low income. In addition, the loan debt load cannot exceed the borrower income by more than 41 percent, and like the FHA loan, the borrower will be required to purchase mortgage insurance.

TIMELY ADVICE IF YOU HAVE NOT BOUGHT A HOUSE YET

If you have *not* bought a house yet, make sure you buy a house *within your own means*. I can't stress it hard enough.

With leverage, many people are buying houses that are much more expensive and ambitious than what they really need or, for that matter, can afford. Just because the lender has approved you to buy a certain house does not necessarily mean you should buy it. Buying a home can be your biggest, most ambitious, and expensive undertaking in your lifetime. Be wise about it, and it will save you a lot of money and aggravation down the years.

Remember, when you begin your house-hunting journey, your goal *should not* be to buy the *biggest* house you can afford, but rather to buy a house you can enjoy and still be financially responsible for life's other financial needs such as funding your children's education and saving for unexpected expenses and your retirement.

Choose a house in a nice neighborhood with great schools and conveniences but at the same time allows you to live a financially comfortable life and not being strapped for cash on a monthly basis. Buying below your means will ensure that you are in charge of your mortgage and of your other financial responsibilities and that it never gets the better of you.

CHAPTER 2 - WHY YOU SHOULD PAY OFF YOUR MORTGAGE DEBT FAST

This would be a much better world if more married couples were as deeply in love as they are in debt.
Earl Wilson

DEFINITION OF A MORTGAGE

According to Wikipedia, "A mortgage loan or simply mortgage is used either by purchasers of real property to raise funds to buy real estate or alternatively by existing property owners to raise funds for any purpose while putting a lien on the property being mortgaged. A mortgage can also be described as 'a borrower giving consideration in the form of collateral for a benefit (loan).'"[6]

US MORTGAGE STATISTICS

Mortgage debt is one of the primary debt obligations many people will take during their lifetime to buy a home, recreational property, investment property, or any property or combination of properties, for that matter. It is an instrument of leverage that allows a person to leverage a small down payment into purchasing a much more expensive property. Traditionally, the expected and typical down payment for a home purchase was 20 percent. However, with the rapid increase in home values in recent years, it is not always realistic, especially for a first-time home buyer, to be able to come with a 20 percent down payment. That is why FHA, VA, and mortgage insurers came up with creative products to meet lower down payment needs. Today in the US, the average down payment amount for first-time buyers range between 5 and 10 percent.[5]

The median down payment on single family homes and condos purchased with financing in the first quarter of 2018 was $16,750, down 4 percent from $17,500 in the previous quarter but still up 27 percent from $13,207 in the first quarter of 2017.[7]

According to the Federal Housing Finance Agency, the average loan amount for all loans in the US was $312,900 in April 2018.[8] According to the FHFA, the average interest rate on all mortgage loans was 4.49 percent.[8]

WHY YOU SHOULD PAY OFF YOUR MORTGAGE AS QUICKLY AS YOU CAN?

WHAT HAPPENS ON A 30-YEAR AMORTIZATION LOAN

Let's see what happens when you take a $313,000 mortgage for 30 years at 4.5 percent with a 30-year amortization. If you make no additional payments on this mortgage, here is what happens:

Your monthly mortgage payment is $1,585.93. Therefore, in a year, you are paying $1,585.93 x 12 = $19,031.16.

Here is a table that summarizes what happens within the *first five years:*

30-Year Amortization

	Total Payments	Total Interest	Total Principal	Percent of Principal Payment
Year 1	$19,031.16	$13,981.70	$5,049.46	26.50%
Year 2	$38,062.32	$27,731.42	$10,330.90	27.10%
Year 3	$57,093.48	$41,238.53	$15,854.95	27.80%
Year 4	$76,124.64	$54,491.86	$21,632.78	28.40%
Year 5	$95,155.80	$67,479.76	$27,676.04	29.1%

Do you see what happens here?

In the first five years, *only* about 29 percent of your payments goes to pay your principal down. The rest, about 71 percent of your payments, goes to pay *interest!*

Almost three-fourths of your payments in the first five years go toward interest!

Here is the breakdown for the first five years between total payments, total interest, and total principal paid on a 30-year amortization loan:

First Five Years on a 30-year Amortization Loan

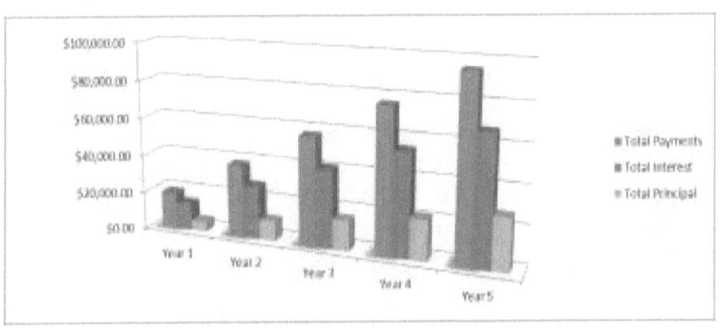

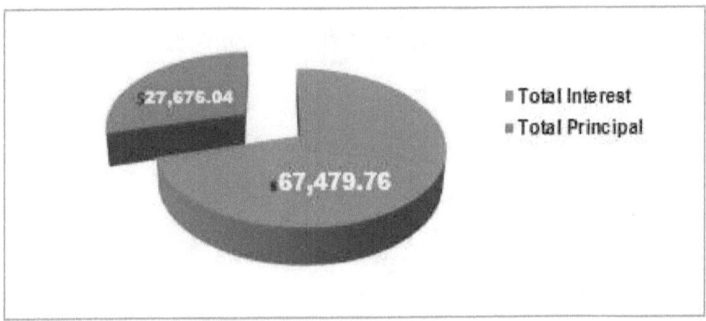

Here is what happens for the duration of the loan (30 years):

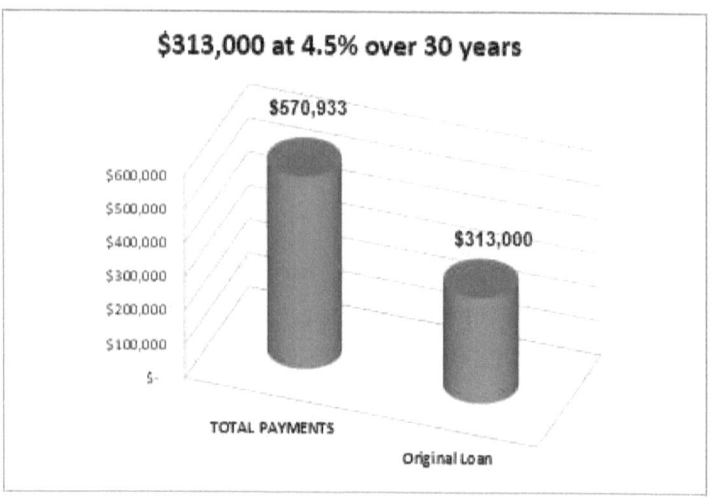

Do you see how we spend our hard-earned money to make the financial institutions wealthy?

In 30 years, the borrower will pay a total of $570,933 on a $313,000 mortgage.

This is *1.824 times* the original amount they borrowed.

In 30 years, the borrower will pay $257,933.01 in interest payments *alone!*

What an *expensive* price we pay for this home!

WHAT HAPPENS ON A 15-YEAR AMORTIZATION

The percentage of principal paid over a five-year period with the same mortgage amount amortized over 15 years is somewhat better. If you make no additional payments on this mortgage, this is what happens:

Your monthly mortgage payment is $2,394.43. Therefore, in a year, you are paying $2,394.43 x 12 = $28,733.16.

Here is a table that summarizes what happens within the first five years on a 15-year amortization loan.

15-Year Amortization				
	Total Payments	Total Interest	Total Principal	Percent of Principal Payment
Year 1	$ 28,733.16	$ 13,779.08	$ 14,954.08	52.0%
Year 2	$ 57,466.32	$ 26,871.15	$ 30,595.17	53.2%
Year 3	$ 86,199.48	$ 39,244.70	$ 46,954.78	54.5%
Year 4	$ 114,932.64	$ 50,866.68	$ 64,065.96	55.7%
Year 5	$ 143,665.80	$ 61,702.58	$ 81,963.22	57.1%

The ratios are much better on a 15-year amortization than the ones on a loan with a 30-year amortization. However, that means a much *higher* monthly payment.

First Five Years on a 15-year Amortization Loan

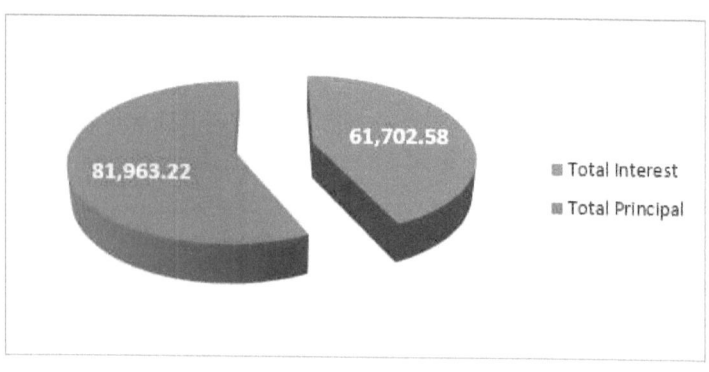

Total Payments on a 15-year Amortization Loan

In 15 years, the borrower will pay a total of $430,997 on a $313,000 mortgage.

This is *1.377 times* the original amount they borrowed. This is *much better* than the 30-year amortization loan, which is 1.824 times the loan amount.

Here are some interesting facts:

- Your monthly payment with a 30-year amortization is $1,585.93.
- Your monthly payment with a 15-year amortization is $2,394.43.
- You basically make $2,394.43 - $1,585.93 = $808.50 extra payment per month.
- Over five years, we are paying $808.50 x 60 = $48,510 *more* on the 15-year amortization payment schedule. (We have 60 monthly payments in five years.)
- Although we have made $48,510 more in payment on a 15-year amortization schedule, we have paid down our principal by $54,287.18 or by *additional* $5,777.18.
- After 15 years, we will pay off the 15-year amortization mortgage but still will have a balance of $207,310.98 left to be paid on the 30-year amortized mortgage.

WHAT DOES IT MEAN?

The conclusion from here is that

- The *shorter* the amortization schedule, *the higher* will be the monthly payment,
- The *shorter* the amortization schedule, the *higher* the portion of principal paid with each payment,
- The *shorter* the amortization schedule, the *faster* the loan will be paid off, and
- The *shorter* the amortization schedule, the *less overall total interest payment* one will make:
  - ❖ $117,997 total interest on a 15-year amortization loan
  - ❖ **$257,931 total interest on a 30-year amortization loan**

This becomes very significant after 10 or 15 years.

POINTS TO REMEMBER

- The monthly payment on a 30-year amortization loan will be the *lowest*.
- You will pay the *most* amount of interest the longer the loan term is. Therefore, you will pay much more interest on 30-year term loan as opposed to a 15- or 20-year term loan.

- After 15 years of a mortgage loan with a 30-year term, you will pay only about 34 percent of the mortgage debt and still will have to go for another 15 years of payments.

But wait a second, you say.

Can you do anything to reduce the amount of interest you pay on your mortgage without reducing the amortization and increasing my monthly payment?

The answer is *yes*, you absolutely can!

In the following chapters, I will show you how to cut the amount of interest you pay by thousands of dollars and how to pay off your mortgage in just a few short years instead of in 30 years *without* changing your payment amount or modifying your payment amount in any way.

I hope that you, after reading this chapter, gain appreciation as to how important it is to *pay your mortgage as fast as possible* and *how much a mortgage really costs us*. It chains us for many years, and it robs us and our family from a big chunk of our earnings.

Please go to my website at www.financial-wisdom.net and download my complementary Microsoft Excel mortgage spreadsheet so you can put your own particular mortgage numbers and see exactly your own specific situation.

Now let's dive into a new concept that will help us explain how to go about paying your mortgage in a few short years.

CHAPTER 3 - HOW TO PAY OFF YOUR MORTGAGE IN A FEW SHORT YEARS

Chains of habit are too light to be felt until they are too heavy to be broken.
Warren Buffett

In the previous chapters, we shed some light as to how much money one pays if they stay locked for 30 years with their mortgage. *It's absolutely insane.* Many people do it simply because they either don't know better or because they get into a routine and therefore don't want to leave their comfort zone, learn creative strategies, and/or do something outside their comfort zone. ***You are not that person.* This is why you read this book**.

Okay, so we know we need to do something. The question is *what?*

There are few strategies we can implement such as

- Doubling up on payments
- Making extra payments

    As we have seen earlier, the majority of the earliest mortgage payments will be for interest payment instead of principal reduction on a typical 30-year mortgage loan. Any extra payments that are applied directly to the principal amount will decrease the loan balance and as such decrease the amount of time it will take to pay the loan and the amount of interest paid.

- Paying an extra amount to reduce the loan principal balance at any time or regularly.
- Make biweekly (once every two weeks) payments of half month's payment which will be the equivalent of making 13 months of mortgage repayments in a year instead of 12 payments. (Paying your mortgage every two weeks will mean making 26 half-month payments per year, which is equivalent to

making 13 monthly payments per year instead of 12.)

We will cover these strategies in Chapter 4 because in this chapter, I want to concentrate on the **_best strategy_ to pay off your mortgage** in a few short years.

THE CONCEPT

The concept in its simplest form involves reducing the loan balance of an amortized interest loan with funds borrowed against a revolving debt instrument, which utilizes a simple interest loan along with somewhat rearranging where you deposit your monthly income and pay your expenses.

Instead of depositing your family monthly salary, commission, or bonus compensation in a checking account, we will open a different type of account and make the deposit there, and we will also pay all our expenses from this new account.

Why would we do this?

Keep on reading, and it will become crystal clear.

I also want to introduce you to two new types of accounts. You may or may not have heard of them before: *HELOC* (home equity line of credit) and *PLOC* (personal line of credit) accounts.

Let's delve a little bit into these two accounts so it becomes a bit clearer what they are and how we go about getting them. Then I will teach you how to implement my four-step accelerated mortgage payoff strategy.

HELOC is a loan in which the lender agrees to lend a maximum amount within an agreed period (called a term), where the collateral is the borrower's equity in his or her house.[10]

In simple terms, HELOC is a *revolving* loan borrowed against portion of your home's equity. It is therefore a secured loan, where the security is the property. Revolving loans allow for the loan amount or any portion of it to be withdrawn, repaid in full or in portion, and then redrawn again in any fashion and for any number of times.

HELOC have lower interest rates than other types of unsecured debt such as credit cards or personal loans. HELOC uses the equity in your home, that is, the difference between your home's value and your mortgage balance as collateral.

A lender will lend you a portion of your equity but not the full value of your equity. The portion of equity a lender will lend will depend on timing and the market. However, in general, it will range between 60 to 80 percent of your equity. The HELOC offers you access to a specified amount of money, but you do not have to use any of it. It is a revolving loan, and therefore at any time, the borrower can pay off any remaining balance owed against the HELOC and then borrow it again. HELOC can provide interest-only payments or an amortized payment that includes interest and a portion of the loan balance. We will want an *interest-only* loan as the outstanding balance of the loan will be paid within few months, and an interest loan as opposed to an amortized payment will have lower monthly payments and will be easier on monthly cash flow.

PLOC is unsecured Personal Line of Credit. It is a revolving credit account that gives you the right to draw funds up to the line of credit limit. We will talk more about PLOC later in the chapter.

To implement this system, we will need the following:

- HELOC or PLOC if there's not enough equity in the house
- A Visa card. (I would suggest a bit of market research to find a credit card that will reward you with air miles and/or lower interest rate.) The key is to *pay off the card balance every month*. You have a 30- to 35-day grace period before payment is due. If you pay the balance on time, you will *not* incur any interest charges.
- A mortgage on your property

HERE IS HOW THE FOUR-STEP SYSTEM WILL WORK

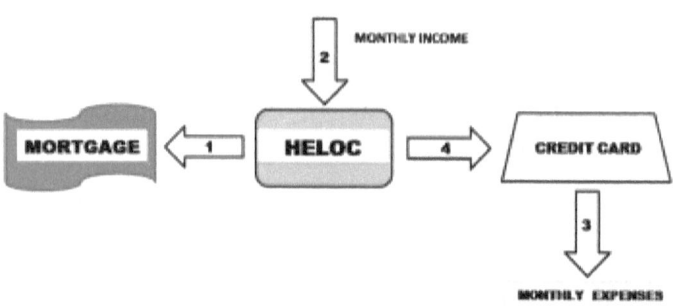

1. Withdraw your HELOC available funds (or a portion of them) to pay down your mortgage principal.

Then do the following monthly:

1. Deposit your monthly income into the HELOC account.
2. Pay your living expenses using a credit card.
3. When the credit card payment is due, pay it from the HELOC.
4. Repeat until the HELOC balance is zero.
5. Increase your HELOC to maximum amount available.
6. Repeat from step one.

Let us use an example to make this process more transparent:

The 2017 National Profile of Home Buyers and Sellers show a national *median* purchase price of $235,000 and a median down payment of 10 percent of the purchase price. With that information, you can calculate a loan size of $211,500.[9]

Now, median is not the same as average. Averages can get skewed by extremely high or low values, but the median gives a representation of where the middle is for a broad range of mortgages. For the examples we use in this book, we will use a rounded mortgage amount of $200,000 at 3.25 percent interest.

In our example, we have the following assumptions:

- A family with net income of $8,000 per month
- Expenses of $5,500 per month
- Home mortgage of $200,000 at 3.25 percent interest amortized over 30 years with 30-year term and a monthly payment of $870.41
- We arrange an *interest-only* HELOC on our home for 35,000 at 5.0 percent interest only for 15 years. (We do not want any loan amortization payments on our HELOC.)

Here is what happens:

- We arrange for our HELOC or PLOC.
- We arrange for a credit card.

Phase 1

1. You transfer $35,000 from the HELOC to pay down your *principal* on the mortgage. Please make sure when you make the payment to your lender that you specify that the payment should *apply to your principal!*
2. Deposit your monthly income of $8,000 into the HELOC account.
3. Pay your monthly expenses of $5,500 from your credit card.
4. Transfer the $5,500 to pay your credit card balance from the HELOC.

➢ Since there is a difference between your income and expenses (in our example, it is $2,500 per month), this money sits in your HELOC account and therefore reduces the HELOC outstanding balance.

➢ After about 14 months, the HELOC balance will go back to zero (14 months x $2500 = $35,000).

➢ Interest on the HELOC is about 35,000 x 5.0% ÷ 12 or $145.83 per month.

Here is a summary of what happens once we put the $35,000 HELOC into the mortgage principal.

HELOC 1: $35,000 (1st Month)

	Original Mortgage	Speedy Mortgage	Savings
Balance	$ 200,000	$ 165,000	-
Total Interest to Be Paid	$ 113,349	$ 67,009	$ 46,341
Total Payments	360	267	93
HELOC	$ 35,000		
Interest Paid	$ 2,188		

*The interest on the HELOC account is 5% simple interest. Therefore, the monthly payment is $145.83. By paying it off by month 15, we pay $2187.45 in interest.

Phase 2

Sixteen months into the mortgage, we take the second HELOC in the amount of $35,000.

Since your HELOC balance is at zero, you transfer $35,000 again from the HELOC to pay down your *principal* on the mortgage. When you make the payment, please make sure to request your lender that the payment will apply to your principal!.

Here is a summary:

HELOC 2: $35,000 (16 month into the mortgage)

	Original Mortgage	Speedy Mortgage	Savings
Balance	$ 194,632	$ 123,183	-
Total Interest to Be Paid	$ 105,319	$ 32,800	$ 72,519
Total Payments	344	195	149
HELOC	$ 35,000		
Interest Paid	$ 2,188		

*The interest on the HELOC account is 5% simple interest. Therefore, the monthly payment is $145.83. By paying it off by month 15, we pay $2187.45 in interest.

Phase 3

Thirty-two months into the mortgage, we take the third HELOC in the amount of $80,000. Since we paid the outstanding mortgage balance substantially, the equity at this point is over $120,000, and therefore we can negotiate with the bank/lender to increase our HELOC.

It is also a good opportunity to check the market and perhaps negotiate a better interest rate. Also, your track record of making prompt payments on your credit card and HELOC builds a better credit score. You are now having a higher equity position in the property, and your credit score is much better, so you are in an excellent position to negotiate a higher HELOC and perhaps even get a better rate.

Let's continue with our example. Let's assume we've negotiated a higher HELOC of $80,000. We now transfer $80,000 from the HELOC to pay down the mortgage *principal* in month 32.

Here is a summary of how it will look:

HELOC 3: $80,000 (32 month into the mortgage)

	Original Mortgage	Speedy Mortgage	Savings
Balance	$ 189,026	$ 34,417	-
Total Interest to Be Paid	$ 96,983	$ 2,347	$ 94,636
Total Payments	328	74	254
HELOC	$ 80,000		
Interest Paid	$ 12,333		

* The interest on the HELOC account is 5% simple interest. Therefore the monthly payment is $145.83. By Paying it off in 37 months, we pay $12,333.33 in interest.

Using this systematic approach, we will pay this mortgage in 74 months or six years and two months.

Here is a summary of how much money we have saved:

Look at these savings

	Total Interest Paid
HELOC	$ 16,708
Speedy Mortgage	$ 14,306
TOTAL	31,014
Original Mortgage	$ 113,349
Savings	**$ 82,335**

Without the interest payments on the HELOC, we would save $94,636. However, since we paid interest on the money we borrowed from the HELOC, the total savings are $82,335. We also will pay the mortgage in 74 months, saving 254 months of payments.

Do you see how *awesome* and rewarding this is? Can you see the huge saving in time and in money by shifting the debt between the mortgage, which is an amortized loan, and the HELOC, which is a simple interest loan?

Bear in mind that I do not account for the fact that in six years your income has most likely gone up. If you have more income, you can pay your debt even faster by applying additional payments once in a while.

We will cover some of these strategies in the next chapters.

Here is a summary of the HELOC payment strategy on this particular example:

HELOC 1: $35,000 (1st Month)

	Original Mortgage	Speedy Mortgage	Savings
Balance	$ 200,000	$ 165,000	-
Total Interest to Be Paid	$ 113,349	$ 67,009	$ 46,341
Total Payments	360	267	93
HELOC		$ 35,000	
Interest Paid		$ 2,188 *	

*The interest on the HELOC account is 5% simple interest. Therefore, the monthly payment is $145.83. By paying it off by month 15, we pay $2187.45 in interest.

HELOC 2: $35,000 (16 month into the mortgage)

	Original Mortgage	Speedy Mortgage	Savings
Balance	$ 194,632	$ 123,183	-
Total Interest to Be Paid	$ 105,319	$ 32,800	$ 72,519
Total Payments	344	195	149
HELOC		$ 35,000	
Interest Paid		$ 2,188	

*The interest on the HELOC account is 5% simple interest. Therefore, the monthly payment is $145.83. By paying it off by month 15, we pay $2187.45 in interest.

HELOC 3: $80,000 (32 month into the mortgage)

	Original Mortgage	Speedy Mortgage	Savings
Balance	$ 189,026	$ 34,417	-
Total Interest to Be Paid	$ 96,983	$ 2,347	$ 94,636
Total Payments	328	74	254
HELOC		$ 80,000	
Interest Paid		$ 12,333	

* The interest on the HELOC account is 5% simple interest. Therefore the monthly payment is $145.83. By Paying it off in 37 months, we pay $12,333.33 in interest.

The above examples show you how the mechanics of this system work.

Let us do a bit of sensitivity analysis. In other words, let's see different situations and their impact. The table below reflects a $200,000 loan with a 30-year amortization and the same principal repayment schedule of

- $35,000 in month one,
- $35,000 in month 16, and
- $80,000 in month 32.

If you recall our example, use a 3.25 percent on a 30-year amortization in the amount of $200,000. We would pay the mortgage off in 74 months, saving $82,335. Here is our monthly payment and how quickly we will pay the mortgage if the mortgage is at different interest rates.

Interest	Monthly Payments	Paid Off in Month	# of Payments Saved
3.25%	$ 870.41	74	286
4.25%	$ 983.88	70	290
5.25%	$1,104.41	66	294
6.25%	$1,231.43	63	297

As you can see, the higher the interest rate, the higher will be the monthly payments and therefore the quicker the loan will be paid off.

Your situation might be different. You might have higher or lower mortgage. You might have more or less equity in the property. You might pay more or less interest on your mortgage. Perhaps your income is higher or lower. Whatever is your situation, once you understand how this process works, you can download the free Microsoft Excel spreadsheet from our website

www.financial-wisdom.net to map your own situation.

IN CASE YOU DON'T HAVE ENOUGH EQUITY IN THE HOUSE

Now, in case you don't have enough equity in the house, we can use an *unsecured personal line of credit (PLOC),* to help us pay the mortgage quickly.

What is PLOC?

PLOC or Personal Line Of Credit is a revolving credit account which gives you the right to draw funds up to the line of credit limit. It's similar to a personal credit card because it allows you to borrow funds as needed. Personal lines of credit are usually unsecured loans, which means that there is no collateral securing the loan. The funds can be accessed through debit cards or line-of-credit checks.

Personal lines of credit can be issued for different amounts depending on your individual circumstances, but like a credit card, they consider your credit history, employment, and the ability to pay. Personal lines of credit generally permit you to draw any amount as long as it's below the line of credit limit.

Alternatively, if you are a business owner, you can apply for business lines of credit. It is the same idea. (This is what I used in my situation. Please see Chapter 7.)

The main advantage of the personal line of credit is its *flexibility* and the fact it is unsecured. Money can be drawn and paid off repeatedly, as it's a revolving line.

PLOC provides a major advantage over more traditional fixed-term personal loans such as mortgages, which are paid out in one lump sum, and once you make a payment, the money cannot be withdrawn again. There are also fewer restrictions on what a personal line of credit may be used for, unlike mortgages.

The idea here is the same. We borrow money from a *revolving and simple interest account* to pay the amortized loan amount, which is *much more expensive.*

In the process, we build equity, we build a better credit score, we pay off our mortgage years sooner, and we save lots of money that will help us build a better financial future.

Let's look at an example to see how this situation unfolds:

We are using the same assumptions as before. However, in this example, the borrower *does not* have enough equity in the house to borrow on a HELOC, so we would look in the market for an unsecured PLOC.

Do some homework here. The better your credit history, the easier for you to arrange for a favorable PLOC.

Tip: make sure the PLOC *is simple interest LOC only.*

Obviously, we will not be able to borrow as much as we would on the HELOC (remember, the HELOC is secured against our home equity), and the interest we will pay on the PLOC will be higher than the one we will pay on the HELOC. However, the approach is very similar to the previous scenario. Instead of using the available funds in our HELOC, we will use the funds in our PLOC.

Here is how the system will work:

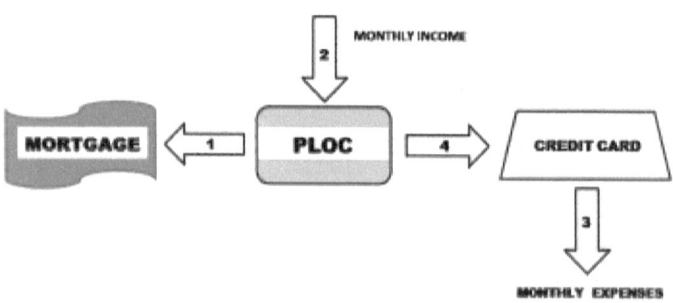

1. Withdraw your PLOC available funds (or a portion of them) to pay down your mortgage principal.

Then do the following monthly:

1. Deposit your monthly income into the PLOC account.
2. Pay your living expenses using a credit card.
3. When the credit card payment is due, pay it from the PLOC.
4. Repeat step 2 until the PLOC balance is zero.
5. Check to see if you have enough equity in your property to arrange a HELOC. If not, repeat from step 1.

Let us use the same example as we've done previously to make this process more transparent.

In our example, we have the following assumptions:

- A family with net income of $8,000 per month
- Expenses of 5,500 per month
- Home mortgage of $200,000 at 3.25 percent interest amortized over 30 years. The monthly payment is $870.41.
- We arrange an *interest-only* PLOC for $25,000 at 8 percent interest only for 10 years. (We do not want any loan amortization payments on our PLOC.)

Here is what happens. Once we have arranged for our PLOC,

1. We withdraw $25,000 from the PLOC to pay down the *principal* on the mortgage. When you make the payment to your lender, please make sure you specify that the payment should *apply to your principal!*
2. We deposit the monthly income of $8,000 into the PLOC account.
3. We pay the monthly expenses of $5,500 from the credit card.
4. We transfer the $5,500 to pay the credit card balance from the PLOC.

➢ Since there is a difference between the income and expenses (in our example, it is $2,500 per month), this money accumulates in your PLOC account (instead of sitting in a checking account earning next to nothing in interest). Therefore, the excess of funds reduces the outstanding PLOC balance every month.
➢ After about 10 to 11 months, the PLOC balance will go back to zero.
➢ 11 months x $2500 = $27,500, which will pay for the $25,000 + interest.
➢ Interest on the PLOC is about $25,000 x 8.0% ÷ 12 = $166.67 per month. (It is actually less

because our balance is going down every month by about $2,500.)

Here is a summary of what happens:

Phase 1

1. We transfer $25,000 from the PLOC to pay down the principal amount on the mortgage. When you make the payment to your lender, please make sure you specify that the payment should apply to your principal!
2. We deposit the monthly income of $8,000 into the PLOC account.
3. We pay the monthly expenses of $5,500 from the credit card.
4. We transfer the $5,500 to pay the credit card balance from the PLOC.

Here is a summary of what happens once we put the $25,000 PLOC into the mortgage principal.

PLOC 1: $25,000 (1st Month)

	Original Mortgage	Speedy Mortgage	Savings
Balance	$ 200,000	$ 175,000	
Total Interest to Be Paid	$ 113,349	$ 78,229	$ 35,120
Total # of Payments	360	291	69
PLOC	$ 25,000		
Interest paid	$ 1,667 *		

* The interest on the PLOC account is 8% simple interest. Therefore the monthly payment is $166.67 By Paying it off by month 10, we pay $1,666.70 in interest.

Phase 2

Twelve months into the mortgage, we withdraw $25,000 for the *second time* from the PLOC.

Since your PLOC balance is at zero, you transfer $25,000 again from the PLOC to pay down your *principal* on the mortgage. When you make the payment, please make sure to request your lender that the payment will *apply to your principal!*

Here is a summary:

PLOC 2: $25,000 (12 Months into the Mortgage)

	Original Mortgage	Speedy Mortgage	Savings
Balance	$ 195,996	$ 145,241	-
Total Interest to Be Paid	$ 107,440	$ 48,744	$ 58,696
Total # of Payments	348	224	124
PLOC	$ 25,000		
Interest paid	$ 1,667 *		

*The interest on the PLOC account is 8% simple interest. Therefore the monthly payment is $166.67 By Paying it off by month 10, we pay $1,666.70 in interest.

Phase 3

Twenty-four months into the mortgage, we withdraw $25,000 for the *third time* from the PLOC.

Since your PLOC balance is at zero, you transfer $25,000 again from the PLOC to pay down your *principal* on the mortgage. Please make sure when you make the payment to request your lender that the payment will apply to your principal!

Here is a summary:

PAY OFF YOUR MORTGAGE IN 3 YEARS

HELOC 3: $25,000 (24 Months into the Mortgage)

	Original Mortgage	Speedy Mortgage	Savings
Balance	$ 191,859	$ 114,430	–
Total Interest to Be Paid	$ 101,121	$ 27,595	$ 73,526
Total # of Payments	336	164	172
PLOC	$ 25,000		
Interest paid	$ 1,667		

* The interest on the PLOC account is 8% simple interest. Therefore the monthly payment is $166.67 By Paying it off by month 10, we pay $1,666.70 in interest.

Phase 4

Thirty-six months into the mortgage, we now build enough equity in our property. We will be able to apply for and negotiate with the bank/lender a HELOC of $75,000 since we paid the outstanding mortgage balance substantially.

We now transfer $75,000 from the HELOC to pay down the mortgage *principal* in month 36. Here is a summary of how it will look:

HELOC 4: $75,000 (36 Months into the Mortgage)

	Original Mortgage	Speedy Mortgage	Savings
Balance	$ 187,587	$ 32,603	–
Total Interest to Be Paid	$ 94,936	$ 5,819	$ 89,118
Total # of Payments	324	53	271
HELOC	$ 75,000		
Interest paid	$ 10,625		

*The interest on the HELOC account is 5% simple interest. Therefore, the monthly payment is $312.50. By paying it off in 34 months, we pay $10,625.00 in interest

Using this systematic approach, we will pay this mortgage in 76 months or six years and four months.

Here is a summary of how much money we have saved:

Look at these savings

	Total Interest Paid
PLOC	$ 5,000
HELOC	$ 10,625
Speedy Mortgage	$ 15,760
Total	31,385
Original Mortgage	$ 113,349
Savings	$ 81,965

Without the interest payments on the PLOC and HELOC, we would save $89,118. However, since we pay interest on the money we've borrowed from the PLOC and HELOC, the total savings are $81,965.

Here is a summary of the PLOC system:

PLOC 1: $25,000 (1st Month)

	Original Mortgage	Speedy Mortgage	Savings
Balance	$ 200,000	$ 175,000	-
Total Interest to Be Paid	$ 113,349	$ 78,229	$ 35,120
Total # of Payments	360	291	69
PLOC	$ 25,000		
Interest paid	$ 1,667 *		

* The interest on the PLOC account is 8% simple interest. Therefore the monthly payment is $166.67 By Paying it off by month 10, we pay $1,666.70 in interest.

PLOC 2: $25000 (12 Months into the Mortgage)

	Original Mortgage	Speedy Mortgage	Savings
Balance	$ 195,996	$ 145,241	-
Total Interest to Be Paid	$ 107,440	$ 48,744	$ 58,696
Total # of Payments	348	224	124
PLOC	$ 25,000		
Interest paid	$ 1,667 *		

* The interest on the PLOC account is 8% simple interest. Therefore the monthly payment is $166.67 By Paying it off by month 10, we pay $1,666.70 in interest.

HELOC 3: $25,000 (24 Months into the Mortgage)

	Original Mortgage	Speedy Mortgage	Savings
Balance	$ 191,859	$ 114,430	–
Total Interest to Be Paid	$ 101,121	$ 27,595	$ 73,526
Total # of Payments	336	164	172
PLOC	$ 25,000		
Interest paid	$ 1,667 *		

* The interest on the PLOC account is 8% simple interest. Therefore the monthly payment is $166.67 By Paying it off by month 10, we pay $1,666.70 in interest.

HELOC 4: $75,000 (36 Months into the Mortgage)

	Original Mortgage	Speedy Mortgage	Savings
Balance	$ 187,587	$ 32,603	–
Total Interest to Be Paid	$ 94,936	$ 5,819	$ 89,118
Total # of Payments	324	53	271
HELOC	$ 75,000		
Interest paid	$ 10,625		

*The interest on the HELOC account is 5% simple interest. Therefore, the monthly payment is $312.50. By paying it off in 34 months, we pay $10,625.00 in interest

The numbers in the examples above will be most likely very different than your own numbers. However, they illustrate the mechanics of how to pay the mortgage years upon years sooner. Bear in mind that in this example, I do not account for the fact that in six years your income most likely has gone up. If you have more income, you can pay your debt even faster by applying additional payments once in a while. I know it's extreme, and I am not one who promotes complete lifestyle starvation, but you will agree that by tightening the belt for few years, the benefits will greatly outweigh the drawbacks and will last for a lifetime without debt and financial stress. *Your family deserves it.* In Chapter 6, we will show you how much better financially you and your family will be down the road.

A FEW CAVEATS TO REMEMBER:

- HELOC and PLOC are non-deductible interest expense like a payment of a mortgage interest is. The IRS website states: "The Tax Cuts and Jobs Act of 2017, enacted December 22, suspends from 2018 until 2026 the deduction for interest paid on home equity loans and lines of credit, unless they are used to buy, build, or substantially improve the taxpayer's home that secures the loan."[11] It means that in general, HELOC or PLOC are *not* a tax-deductible expense unless the funds have been used to improve the home. To evaluate your particular circumstance, I would recommend that you consult with a qualified CPA.
- When interest rates increase, the variable rate on the personal line of credit also increases.
- PLOC requires reasonably good credit score and stable income to qualify.
- The mortgage calculation example *does not* include the cost of insurance and taxes. These costs can add an additional component to the monthly expenses.
- Some lenders will charge fees in order to make additional payments on your mortgage.
- My calculation assumes a particular situation and is for explanatory and illustrative purposes.

To determine your own situation, start by downloading our free Microsoft Excel mortgage amortization spreadsheet from www.financial-wisdom.net and put your own mortgage numbers.

- This system assumes the monthly income leaves an excess of $2,500 per month. If your situation is different, it will affect the speed of paying the loans.

We know life is not perfect, and I am not suggesting this system will work for everyone. It really depends on your personal circumstances, your monthly income, expenses, and your credit history, to name some. However, once you are aware of this system, even if you do not qualify to do it at this point, you will be qualified to implement this system at one point later in your life. I truly believe that once you are aware of this method and once you make up your mind to make it work for you, you will find a way to implement this type of system in your own circumstances sooner than later.

I encourage you to figure out your own specific situation and download the free Microsoft Excel mortgage spreadsheet. You will be able to see exactly your situation, and you can try different scenarios using your own mortgage numbers.

SOME TIPS TO HELP YOU SET THIS IN MOTION:

- Check local as well as national banks to see who will give you a better deal.
- Set your HELOC like a checking account with a debit card so it is easy to take or deposit money into the account.
- Some local banks contact the HELOC borrower every time there is a payment or expense payment from the account. That can be a big nuisance. That is why it's easier and it makes more sense to charge all monthly living expenses to a credit card and pay the card once per month from the HELOC or PLOC.
- When applying for a credit card, make sure the card provides you with low introductory interest rate as well as other benefits such as cash back, air miles, etc. If you use your card to accumulate air miles like I do, it will add up rather quickly and let you benefit from free flights, paying for hotel stays, etc.
- Negotiate your HELOC or PLOC terms. If you have a good credit history, you can negotiate better interest rates for your HELOC or PLOC.

As a first step, do your budget and see where your numbers are going and how much you can have as extra each month. Once you put it on paper and monitor it, you realize where your numbers are going and where you can save extra money each month.

Once you know your numbers and you commit to pay your mortgage sooner, you will be on your path. This method is creative and resourceful. For some of you reading this book, it might not be relevant, and if this is the case, every little extra payment on your mortgage principal balance will save you money in the long run. Chapter 4 will show you other ways to pay your mortgage sooner and save time and money. If you are in a position to implement this four-step system and if you make a commitment to implement it, your debt reduction progress will be faster and very rewarding.

CHAPTER 4 - HOW TO ACCELERATE YOUR MORTGAGE PAYMENT WITH OTHER OPTIONS

The caliber of your future will be determined by the choices you make today.
Anthony O'Neal

Paying extra on your mortgage debt is always a good idea. Every extra dollar one pays to reduce the principal balance will shave time off the home loan and save thousands of dollars in interest charges.

Here are a few ideas:

SET UP BIWEEKLY PAYMENTS

Instead of making 12 monthly payments per year, the biweekly payment plan provides for one payment every two weeks, which adds up to 13 payments per year. We have 12 months in a year, so if you make one payment per month, you will end up paying 12 payments per year on your mortgage. However, if you will divide your monthly cost by half and make a payment every two weeks, the 26 half-monthly payments will add up to 13 monthly payments per year.

In some cases, switching to biweekly payments is as simple as asking your lender to alter your current payment plan. However, not many lenders allow customers to switch to biweekly payments at no charge. In order to prevent any cost utilizing this idea, you can have the half-monthly payment money transferred automatically from your checking account to a savings account every two weeks, and then at the end of the month, you transfer this money to your lender. By the end of the year, you'll have made 26 half payments, which add up to 13 monthly payments, making one full extra payment per year. That extra payment per year can knock several years off a 30-year mortgage, depending on the loan's interest rate. For example, a $200,000, 30-year mortgage with an interest rate of 5 percent would cost $186,513 in interest with the traditional 12 payments a year. However, make the equivalent of 13 monthly payments every year, and the loan will be paid off in 25 years and four months, saving almost five years of payments. You will pay only $153,814 in interest—a savings of $32,699.

Here is a table summarizing the *interest-saving cost* at *different interest rates* between making a 12 (monthly payment schedule) or 13 payments per year (biweekly payment schedule) on a $200,000, 30-year mortgage term and amortization at the following interest rates:

Interest	12 Monthly Payments/Year	13 Monthly Payments/Year	Interest Payment Savings	Time Savings
3.5%	$123,312	$106,346	$16,966	3 years and 8 month
4.0%	$143,739	$122,266	$21,473	4 years
4.5%	$164,814	$138,115	$26,699	4 years and 3 month
5.0%	$186,513	$153,814	$32,699	4 years and 7 month
5.5%	$208,807	$169,273	$39,534	4 years and 11 month
6.0%	$231,677	$184,395	$47,282	5 years and 3 month

Most people would never guess that making *one* extra mortgage payment each year could save them *so much money*.

Once you look at these numbers and you see how much money you can save and how many years you can shave off your mortgage, I am sure you will give this idea a serious consideration.

ADD AN EXTRA SUM EACH MONTH

Each month or every other month, add a set amount to your regular mortgage payment. Even an extra $50 or $60 per month adds quite substantially in the long run. For instance, if you pay a monthly loan an extra $50 per month on a $200,000 30-year mortgage with an interest rate of 5 percent, you will save $20,779 over the life of the loan, saving you 36 monthly payments.

How would you get an extra $50 to $100 per month? Here are a few suggestions:

o Pack your own lunches.
o Cancel your gym membership if you don't use it.
o Buy or lease a cheaper car (just for a few years).
o Share a ride with colleagues if you drive to work. You will save on gas and parking cost.
o Rent your basement (if applicable).
o Consider how much you pay on personal trainers, protein shakes, supplements, golf, skiing, and other sports. Many don't consider how much they spend because they either don't pay attention to it or because they believe that they are spending money on something healthy or something they love. It's all a question of priorities. If you make a commitment to getting out of debt faster, cutting back what you spend

on some hobbies, even just for a while, may be a great option to consider.
- ○ Change your cable plan.
- ○ Change your internet plan.
- ○ Cut your landline.
- ○ Review and shop around for your car and home insurance policies.
- ○ Renegotiate your bank fees.
- ○ Sell what you don't need.
- ○ Cut unused subscriptions.
- ○ Cut game rentals.
- ○ Avoid impulsive spending, especially at the grocery store.
- ○ Make yourself a budget. It will open your eyes to where the money goes and where you can save.
- ○ Start a side hustle online.
- ○ Use coupons. You can request them from many grocery chains or from coupon websites.

Did you ever consider that simply paying $50 per month will save you so much money?

Now what if you make $75 or $100 per month?

Using the same example as before, a $200,000 30-year mortgage with an interest rate of 5 percent will save you the following amounts over the life of the loan:

Monthly extra	Interest payment Savings	Time Savings
$ 50	$ 20,779	2 years and 10 month
$ 75	$ 29,384	4 years and 1 month
$ 100	$ 37,070	5 years and 2 month
$ 125	$ 43,986	6 years and 2 month
$ 150	$ 50,247	7 years and 1 month

Different interest rates or different loan amounts will produce different amounts for the above numbers. Regardless, this table is an eye-opener and really echoes on the fact that paying *any extra* amount on your principal balance can make a *substantial* difference in the amount of interest you pay and the amount of time it takes to pay your loan.

CUT THE AMORTIZATION ON YOUR LOAN

In general, if a person can afford to pay higher monthly payments, then a shorter amortization period will certainly reduce the amount of interest and the time frame of the loan. (See Chapter 2 for a comparison between a 15- and 30-year amortized loans. In addition, a 15-year mortgage will most likely have a lower interest rate. Cutting the amortization schedule on a loan will command a larger monthly payment. However, at the same time it will accelerate the mortgage payment time frame because a larger portion of principal repayment is made with each payment.

Just be aware that once you set this loan in motion, your monthly payments will stay the same for the duration of the loan, so if a 15-year amortization loan payment stretches your budget to the hilt, think twice about it. You can use other ways to cut your amortization throughout the payment process with making a periodic extra payment, etc.

USE YOUR TAX REFUND TO PAY DOWN YOUR PRINCIPAL

Are you getting a refund this year? If you are, you can use your refund or portion of it to pay down the principal of your mortgage. Your regularly scheduled payments won't change, but making a practice of this habit will make a significant difference.

How much of a difference?

Well, let's consider we apply a portion refund of, say, $500 per year. On a *$200,000, 30-year mortgage* with an *interest rate of 5 percent,* you will save *$17,004* over the life of the loan, and you will pay off your loan in 27 years and eight months instead of 30 years.

What if we pay more?

Using the same example as before, a $200,000, 30-year mortgage with an interest rate of 5 percent will save you the following amounts over the life of the loan:

Yearly Extra Payment	Interest Payment Savings	# of Payment Savings
$ 400	$ 13,887	23
$ 500	$ 17,004	28
$ 750	$ 24,268	**40**
$ 1,000	$ 30,867	52
$ 1,250	$ 36,892	**62**

Any time you make extra mortgage payments, it goes straight to reducing the principal balance. With a lower principal balance, you are charged less interest with each payment, and therefore you pay your mortgage faster. A larger portion of your payment goes toward your principal and less to interest. If you have a long remaining term and/or a very large mortgage size, you might not notice a drastic change in your outstanding mortgage balance initially. However, as the years go by and as you can see from the above example, paying consistently year after year will save you thousands of dollars and save you years in payments.

PUT YOUR RAISE TO WORK

Are you getting a raise in pay this year? If you are, you can use your raise or a portion of it to pay down the principal of your mortgage. Your regularly scheduled payments won't change, but making a practice of this habit will make a significant difference.

How much of a difference?

Well, let's consider we apply a portion of your annual increase of, say, $1500 per year. On a *$200,000, 30-year mortgage* with an *interest rate of 5* percent, you will save *$42,418* over the life of the loan, and you will pay off your loan in exactly 24 years instead of 30 years.

What if we pay more?

Using the same example as before, on a $200,000 30-year mortgage with an interest rate of 5 percent, you will save the following amounts over the life of the loan:

Yearly Extra Payment	Interest Payment Savings	# of Payment Savings
$ 1,500	$ 42,418	72
$ 2,000	$ 52,238	89
$ 2,500	$ 60,682	105
$ 3,000	$ 68,035	119
$ 3,500	$ 74,510	131

Keep in mind that every lender and every mortgage have its own prepayment rules.

To prevent any prepayment penalty, read your mortgage document or contact your mortgage lender before making the payment to make sure it is within the limit of what you are allowed to pay annually.

Paying any extra on your mortgage principal balance is a good idea. However, bear in mind that applying any of the above ways to reduce your mortgage principal will *not* reduce your regular monthly payment or allow you to skip a payment.

Now that you have seen some ways to save money and time on your mortgage, are you ready to pay your mortgage in just three years?

Chapter 5 will show you how.

CHAPTER 5 - HOW TO PAY YOUR MORTGAGE IN AS LITTLE AS THREE YEARS

Measurement is the first step that leads to control and eventually to improvement. If you can't measure something, you can't understand it. If you can't understand it, you can't control it. If you can't control it, you can't improve it.
H. James Harrington

You realize that to achieve a remarkable feat like paying a 30-year mortgage in just three to three and a half years, you will have to make tremendous sacrifices. Not every person will be financially able or willing to do that. However, if you have the financial ability and if you and your spouse (yes, the spouse or partner has to be on board for something that extreme to work) are truly committed to get rid of your home loan and *live mortgage-free in three years*, then here is what you need or aim to do:

In our example, we have the following assumptions:

- A family with net income of $8,000 per month
- Expenses of 5,500 per month
- Home mortgage of $200,000 at 3.25 percent interest amortized over 15 years. The monthly payment is $1,405.34.
- We arrange an *interest-only* HELOC or PLOC on our home for $35,000 at 5 percent interest only for 15 years. (We do not want any loan amortization payments on our HELOC.)

Here is what happens once we have arranged for our HELOC or PLOC:

PHASE 1: HELOC/PLOC 1

1. You transfer $35,000 from the HELOC or PLOC to pay down your *principal* on the mortgage.
2. You deposit your monthly income of $8,000 into the HELOC account.
3. Pay your monthly expenses of $5,500 from your credit card.
4. Transfer the $5,500 to pay your credit card balance from the HELOC.

➤ Since there is a difference between your income and expenses (in our example, it is $2,500 per month), this excess money in your HELOC account reduces the HELOC outstanding balance.

➤ After about 14 months, the HELOC balance will go back to zero (14 months x $2500 = $35,000).

➤ Interest on the HELOC is about 35,000 x 5.0% ÷ 12 or $145.83 per month.

Here is a summary of what happens once we put the $35,000 HELOC into the mortgage principal:

HELOC 1: $35,000 (1st Month)

	Original Mortgage	Speedy Mortgage	Savings
Balance	$ 200,000	$ 165,000	-
Total Interest to Be Paid	$ 52,961	$ 33,990	$ 18,971
Total Payments	180	142	38
HELOC		$ 35,000	
Interest Paid		$ 2,188	

*The interest on the HELOC account is 5% simple interest. Therefore, the monthly payment is $145.83. By paying it off by month 15, we pay $2187.45 in interest.

PHASE 2: HELOC/PLOC 2

Sixteen months into the mortgage, we take HELOC/PLOC 2 for $60,000.

Since your HELOC/PLOC balance is at zero, and your mortgage loan balance was reduced, then you will be able to negotiate a higher HELOC balance for $60,000.

Once you get approved, you transfer $60,000 from the HELOC to pay down your *principal* on the mortgage.

Here is a summary:

HELOC 2: $60,000 (16 month into the mortgage)

	Original Mortgage	Speedy Mortgage	Savings
Balance	$ 185,897	$ 89,448	-
Total Int to be paid	$ 45,084	$ 9,269	$ 35,815
Total Payments	164	86	78
HELOC		$ 60,000	
Interest Paid		$ 6,000	

* The interest on the HELOC account is 5% simple interest. Therefore the monthly payment is $250.0 By Paying it off within 24 month, we pay $6,000 in interest.

PHASE 3: ADDITIONAL MONTHLY PAYMENTS

To accelerate the mortgage payout, you will have to pay additional monthly payments. The following table reflects the extra monthly payment and how long it will take to pay off the mortgage with the following extra monthly payment:

Monthly Extra Payment	Paid off In Month	
$ 500.00	62	5 years and 2 Month
$ 600.00	59	4 years and 11 Months
$ 700.00	56	4 years and 8 Months
$ 800.00	53	4 years and 5 Months
$ 900.00	50	4 years and 2 Months
$ 1,000.00	48	4 years
$ 1,200.00	44	3 years and 8 months
$ 1,400.00	41	3 years and 5 months
$ 1,500.00	40	3 years and 4 months
$ 1,740.00	36	3 years

Paying *$1,740 per month* with this example *will pay off the mortgage in three years.* If one will pay $1,000 extra per month with this example, one will pay off the loan in four years.

Your situation is obviously different, and you will have to crunch your own numbers to see your monthly ability to pay extra on your particular mortgage. The idea reflected throughout this book is that *any* amount one uses to reduce the mortgage balance will pay dividends in terms of interest payment savings and a shorter payout time frame.

A FEW CAVEATS TO REMEMBER

- HELOC and PLOC are non-deductible interest.
- When interest rates increase, the variable rate on the personal line of credit will most likely increase as well.
- PLOC requires reasonably good credit score and stable income to qualify.
- The mortgage calculation example *does not* include the cost of insurance and taxes. These costs can add an additional component to the monthly expenses.
- This calculation *assumes a particular situation* and is for explanatory and illustrative purposes. To determine your own situation, start by loading my free mortgage amortization spreadsheet from www.financial-wisdom.net and input your own situation numbers.
- This system assumes that the monthly income leaves an excess of $2,500 per month after living expenses but *before* the additional monthly payments. To make $1,000 additional payment per month, you will need $3,500 excess income per month.
- Our calculations above assume a mortgage of $200,000 at 3.25 percent interest rate amortized over 15 years. If *any* of these components is

changed, it will affect the time it will take to pay off the mortgage.
- ➢ Many lenders will not allow you to pay above a certain threshold per year. You will need to read your mortgage document to find your lender's prepayment policy.

The examples I use throughout this book are meant primarily to help you visualize how important it is to make *any* extra payment on the mortgage principal balance and what process needs to be implemented to pay your mortgage years sooner.

Your financial situation might be better or worse. However, I firmly believe that now you know how expensive mortgages are, and I truly believe in what Peter Drucker says, "What gets measured gets managed."

The more you look at your mortgage scenario and the more you measure different aspects of paying it sooner, the more likely you will be motivated to find extra money every month to pay your balance more quickly. Paying off your mortgage in few years as opposed to 20, 25, or even 30 years is an achievement that you and your family will get to enjoy for the rest of your life.

In the next chapter, we will look at an interesting situation describing two couples who make the same income and have similar monthly expenses. Seeing how different their situation becomes as the years go by, you'll realize how crucial it is to pay off your mortgage sooner than later and what a financial difference paying your mortgage sooner will make!

CHAPTER 6 - HOW REMARKABLY DIFFERENT WILL BE YOUR FINANCIAL SITUATION IF YOU PAY YOUR MORTGAGE FASTER

It's so easy to continue down the path you're on in life, allowing the feeling of comfort to rule your daily actions... but if you never take calculated risks, you'll . . . find yourself regretting that you never tried.
Ryan Robinson

Let's see the difference of paying off one's mortgage sooner will make as time goes by.

Let's look at two different couples. Both couples live in the same neighborhood. Both have similar lifestyle. Both have two kids of roughly the same age. Both couples have a similar mortgage. One couple is fully committed to pay their mortgage more quickly, while the other couple prefers to indulge in a regular 30-year term and amortization schedule. We will look how different will be their situation over the next decades.

THE SMITHS VERSUS THE JONESES

Jane and Jason Smith are both working. Jason is an electrician running his own company, while his wife Jane is an office manager in a very busy dental clinic. They are in their mid-30s and have two kids, age five and eight. Between them, they bring home $8,000 per month after taxes. They own a suburban house in a nice neighborhood. They have a *$200,000 mortgage* for *30 years* at 3.25 percent with a *30-year amortization*. Their monthly mortgage payments are $870.41.

Debra and Mark Jones are their next-door neighbors. Mark works as a planner for the city where they live, and Debra is working as an admission clerk at the local university. They are also in their mid-30s and have two kids aged four and six. Between them, they bring home $8,000 per month. Their home is very similar to Jane and Jason's house. They have very similar income and expenses to Jane and Jason's. They have a *$200,000 mortgage* for *15 years* at 3.25 percent with a *15-year amortization*. Their monthly mortgage payments are *$1,405.34* per month. The Joneses are also committed to pay their mortgage as fast as possible so they will make an *extra of $550 per month* additional payment. It stretches their budget. They have to make sacrifices and give up some luxuries their neighbors enjoy, but their commitment to pay off their mortgage is the most important.

Here is what we have:

	The Smiths	The Joneses
Mortgage	$ 200,000	$ 200,000
Interest Rate	3.25%	3.25%
Amortization	30 years	15 years
Monthly Payment	$ 870.41	$ 1,405.34

Now the Joneses also decided to pay their mortgage as fast as they can. They understand it will be difficult, but they are committed to pay the mortgage sooner than later and prepared to make the sacrifices to pay their mortgage sooner than 15 years. They also arrange for a HELOC/PLOC of $25,000 and apply it against their principal in month two. After paying the HELOC/PLOC balance with their excess income, they applied for a HELOC in month 16, as they have built already some equity in their home. They now take the new HELOC for $45,000 and apply it against their principal.

Here is a summary of what happened in month two and month 16:

		The Smiths	The Joneses
HELOC/PLOC	Month 2	$ -	$ 25,000
Mortgage Balance	Month 2	$ 199,342	$ 173,270
HELOC/PLOC	Month 16	$ -	$ 45,000
Mortgage Balance	Month 16	$ 194,632	$ 114,932

The Joneses will pay their mortgage in 108 payments or in exactly nine years. It has taken sacrifice for the Jones family to do that, without a doubt. However, the rewards are starting to be seen already.

HERE IS WHAT HAPPENS AS TIME PROGRESSES

Mortgage Balance	The Smiths	The Joneses
Month 24 (2 Years)	$ 191,859	$ 106,096
Month 36 (3 Years)	$ 187,587	$ 92,479
Month 48 (4 Years)	$ 183,173	$ 78,412
Month 60 (5 Years)	$ 178,614	$ 63,881
-		
-		
Month 96 (8 Years)	$ 164,013	$ 17,348
Month 108 (9 Years)	**$ 158,822**	**$ -**

Already by the end of the fifth year, there's an outstanding mortgage balance *difference of $114,733*. At the end of *ninth year,* the Joneses have *paid off* their mortgage, while the Smiths still have another *21 years* of mortgage payments to go and a mortgage balance of *$158,822.*

What a difference!

But this is just the beginning.

Even as it stands here, look at the amazing difference between the two families. By year eight, most likely the income of both families has gone up.

While the Smiths continues to pau their mortgage, The Joneses decide to invest their excess funds into an investing account (maybe 401K to shelter their earnings) once their mortgage has been paid. The Joneses deposit monthly amount similar to the payment of their neighbors ($870 per month) or perhaps even more. The following table reflects what will be the amount of money they've saved until their neighbors, the Smiths, will pay off their mortgage.

Here is a summary:

Value of Different Monthly Deposits in 21 Years at the Following Rates

Monthly Deposit	Annual Return			
	6.00%	7.00%	8.00%	8.50%
$ 870	$ 437,500	$ 496,750	$ 565,812	$ 604,562
$ 1,000	$ 502,874	$ 570,977	$ 650,359	$ 694,899
$ 1,400	$ 704,024	$ 799,368	$ 910,502	$ 972,858
$ 1,500	$ 754,311	$ 856,466	$ 975,538	$1,042,348

* Annualized return of the S&P 500 from 2007 to the end of 2017 (10 years) was 8.21%. (12)
* Annualized return of the S&P 500 from 1997 to the end of 2017 (20 years) was 8.31%. (12)

Depending on the type of return the future deposits will enjoy, the table above shows results for annual interest growth between 6 percent to 8.5 percent.

The annualized return of the S&P 500 from 2007 to the end of 2017 (10 years) was 8.21 percent.[12] The annualized return of the S&P 500 from 1997 to 2017 (20 years) was 8.31 percent.[12]

Of course, there is no guarantee the market will provide the same returns. You can assume any number for that matter. However, the above table takes several interest rate scenarios with different monthly deposits and shows you the accumulation after 21 years.

Here is an example of three funds that represent the S&P 500.[13]

- SPDR S&P 500 ETF (SPY) issuer: State Street Global Advisors. AUM: $280.33 billion.
- iShares Core S&P 500 ETF (IVV) issuer: BlackRock. AUM: $165.13 billion.
- Vanguard S&P 500 ETF (VOO) issuer: Vanguard. AUM: $105.82 billion.

This book does not attempt to teach you how to invest. There are plenty of good books with more qualified people to do just that. However, I just want to open your eyes to some of the possibilities that can transpire.

Look what happens here. By the time the Smiths has just paid off their mortgage, not only the Joneses has been able to pay off their mortgage years sooner, but they also accumulate a *substantial* nest egg.

A FEW CAVEATS TO REMEMBER

- This scenario does not include the tax effect on capital. To see the full effect on your investment portfolio, you should discuss these matters with your tax adviser or a qualified CPA.
- The mortgage calculation example *does not* include the cost of insurance and taxes. These costs can add an additional component to the monthly expenses.
- Some mortgage lenders will charge extra fees to pay off the mortgage earlier. You will need to check your mortgage document to make sure your mortgage has no fees or limitations when making extra payments on the outstanding mortgage balance.
- Inflation will erode the buying power of the eventual retirement funds, but it still represents a whopping retirement fund.

As one can see, the Joneses' financial situation will *be substantially better* than their neighbors. A few sacrifices in the early year and a strong commitment to a better life coupled with this four-step system will make a decisive difference down the road.

Now I know that some people may say, why not just make extra payments against the principal of the mortgage and skip the whole HELOC/PLOC scenario?

You can do that. However, in general people are *not* disciplined, especially if we talk for periods that span a few years. This type of structure builds the discipline into this process and makes it more automatic, therefore ensuring a higher rate of success. In addition, by implementing this process, people build a great credit history and accumulate points with their credit cards so that they can enjoy free travel, cash back, or any other incentive that is provided by their credit cards.

We all know that many times, life gets in the way. However, if you have a formalized process such as the one described in this book, you get off the wagon one month and automatically you are back on.

CHAPTER 7 - MY SPEEDY MORTGAGE PAYOFF STORY

If you want something new, you have to stop doing something old.
Peter Drucker

Here is how I used the same system as described in Chapter 3 to pay off my mortgage on a recreational waterfront property I purchased few years back.

Here are the mechanics.

A few years back, I had some extra funds from my company's operation, and I decided to invest them in a recreational waterfront property. At the time I had a business line of credit for $100,000 to help me with my monthly business payroll and to help bridge slow periods in my business. When I looked at my business budgets and numbers, I noticed that I rarely needed to draw funds against this business LOC except for a couple of occasions.

Knowing how expensive the mortgage was going to cost, I decided to take some funds from my business LOC and apply it against the mortgage principal balance. The business LOC had a variable rate that was tied to the prime rate. My rate was 5.25 percent, and it was a revolving line of credit, meaning I could pay it off and redraw to the full LOC amount anytime.

I read about and visited the Muskoka region, and I fell in love with it. I spend some time searching for a good deal. I finally found a waterfront property for $270,000.

I put $60,000 down payments and took a $210,000 mortgage. I used a Canadian bank (Royal Bank of Canada), and I took a 10-year term and 25-year amortization loan. I was able to negotiate an excellent rate of 4.34 percent. The bank posted rate for a 10-year loan was much higher, but I was able to negotiate a preferred customer rate.

I chose an accelerated biweekly payment of $527.35 every two weeks or the equivalent of $1,142.59 per month ($527.35 x 26 periods ÷ 12 months = $1,142.59 per month).

Here is what we have:

- Mortgage loan: $210,000
- Interest: 4.34 percent
- Amortization = 25 years
- Term: 10 years
- Biweekly payment of $527.35
- There are 650 payment periods to amortize the full loan (25 years x 26 payments per year = 650).

I checked the mortgage document, and I was allowed to pay up to 10 percent of the original principal balance every year. I tried to negotiate a higher percentage of payout per year, but the bank would not budge.

I decided to pay down the mortgage using my business LOC. However, the bank only allowed paying down the mortgage by 10 percent per year. I decided to make the effort to pay $20,000 per year. My business LOC was a simple interest revolving interest at 5.25 percent. The interest cost per month was $87.50. I made a conscious effort to pay off about $2,000 each and every month to reduce the business LOC. I had the cash flow to do it.

Here is what I did:

- I have paid down my mortgage principal by $20,000 from my business LOC in pay period six.
- I have paid down my mortgage principal by $20,000 from my business LOC in pay period 28.

I kept on doing $20,000 payments against my outstanding balance every year.

The following year (in pay period 54 = two years and one month into the loan), I paid an additional $20,000.

> I have paid down my mortgage principal by $20,000 (from my business LOC) in pay period 54.

The following year (in pay period 80 = three years and one month into the loan), I paid an additional $20,000.

> I have paid down my mortgage principal by $20,000 from my business LOC in pay period 80.

My business cash flow was healthy, so I could reduce my business LOC by $2,000 per month plus the $80 or so for interest. I would pay off the $20,000 balance within 10 to 11 months. In addition, I build my equity in the property nicely within the next few months.

In approximately pay period 100 (which is about four years into the loan), I was able to negotiate a substantial HELOC against my equity in the property. I was approved for a revolving HELOC with a simple interest rate of 3.45 percent. Since a HELOC is a secure loan, the interest rate was much better than my business LOC rate of 5.25 percent, therefore reducing my monthly interest payment for my next $20,000 paydown on the mortgage principal balance. (By the way, I negotiated for the bank to pay for the appraisal cost. I had to pay $200 for legal fees.)

In pay period 106, I made another payment of $20,000, but this time, I borrowed it from my HELOC. In pay period 133 (five years and three months into the loan), I made another $20,000 payment against my mortgage balance from my HELOC. My last payment was for $5,000 in pay period 160, which was paid from my HELOC.

So here is a summary:

- ➢ I have paid down my mortgage principal by $20,000 from my HELOC in pay period 106.
- ➢ I have paid down my mortgage principal by $20,000 from my HELOC in pay period 133.
- ➢ I have paid down my mortgage principal by $5,000 from my HELOC in pay period 160.

The last three payments against the mortgage principal balance were made from the HELOC.

The mortgage was *paid off after 224 pay periods* or eight years and seven months and *savings* of *$99,735*.33 in interest payments and *426 biweekly payments* or *savings* of *over 16 years of payments*.

Here is a summary:

- Mortgage loan = $210,000
- Interest = 4.34 percent
- Term = 10 years
- Biweekly payment of $527.35

Payout Schedule	Mortgage Balance	
	Original Mortgage	Speedy Mortgage
20,000 in period 26	$ 205,215	$ 185,215
20,000 in period 28	**$ 204,838**	**$ 164,772**
20,000 in period 54	$ 199,826	$ 138,002
20,000 in period 80	**$ 194,595**	**$ 110,059**
At about period 100	Negotiated My HELOC	
20,000 in period 106	$ 189,134	$ 80,889
20,000 in period 133	$ 183,209	$ 50,028
5,000 in period 160	$ 177,014	$ 32,761
Pay Off Mortgage in Period 224	**$ 160,655**	**$ -**

I must admit that in the beginning the progress seemed slow and the road to mortgage-free property was daunting, but I persevered, and as the years went by, my situation got better and clearer.

Stick to your program. It might not seem to make a very substantial difference initially, but trust the system and continue the course, and soon enough, you will be rewarded tremendously. Also, using this system reduces the temptation to use the extra funds you have elsewhere, and believe you me, if you have extra funds in your account every month, they will go. Very few people will have the discipline to save, especially when you have so many tempting options out there and retirement seems so far away. This is the beauty of this program—*it builds discipline into your routine*. It becomes habitual, so you stick with it, and the program will save you many paying years and thousands in interest payments.

You might ask, how come you did not pay your mortgage faster?

In all honesty, I could have if I paid some extra money every month. I had the right to double up on my payments, but I did not take advantage of it.

Looking back at it, I could have paid the loan in seven years and saved a couple of years of interest payments if I had paid an additional $100 per pay period against the loan principal. If I had paid $200 per pay period against the loan principal, I would have paid the loan in six years.

I don't recall if I had the cash flow at that time, but for certain, I was missing the hindsight.

Well, hindsight is always perfect, and that is the reason I write this book *so you can learn from my experience.*

Crunch your own numbers, do your budget, do your homework, and once you know where you stand financially, discuss it with your partner, agree on a path to take, implement the four-stage system, and pay down your own mortgage as quickly as you possibly can using the techniques I describe in this book. In the beginning, the process seems to almost make very little difference, but I promise you, if you persevere, this program will be a worthwhile journey.

CHAPTER 8 - CONCLUSION

What gets measured gets managed.
Peter Drucker

I want to take this opportunity to thank you for spending your hard-earned money on buying this book and for spending the time to read through it. I hope I have not confused you too much and that the examples I have provided in the book makes this concept clearer.

There are many ways to peel an orange, so to speak, and there are many ways to pay your mortgage faster. Not all the techniques we outline will work for you. Each person has his or her unique situation or circumstances. However, I hope this book has been as insightful to you as it was intuitive for me to put this concept on paper. I certainly hope that you at least have taken from this book the essence of how *expensive* mortgage debt is and that you have learned some techniques to pay off your mortgage faster.

Every additional payment on your principal, no matter how small, is helpful in reducing the time frame of the mortgage and the amount of interest one pays. I can't stress this enough, especially to young people, how quickly time goes by and how important are budgeting and having your finger on the pulse of your finances.

Unfortunately, the big banks are *not* our friends when it comes to mortgage lending. We need them to help us finance our leveraged home purchase. However, at the same time, we need to understand that we are their customers and that their ultimate responsibility is to make a profit for their shareholders. This is in complete contradiction to our own goals of making sure each of our hard-earned dollar does not feed the wallets of covetous lenders. *Do your homework.* Re-evaluate your financial priorities. Take a fresh look at what is *important to you.* Look at the different options you have, make a budget, and review the numbers often so that you can be in a position to know firsthand about your financial situation—where you can cut things off and how you can make your dollars go the farthest. If you do, I assure you that you will be in a much more secure position later in your life. Remember Peter Drucker's famous saying, "What gets measured gets managed," which is so very true.

Once you decide to make any resolution in your financial destiny, make sure that getting rid of your mortgage debt is a very high priority.

Before I go, I want to challenge you to be different. Reading this book opens your eyes, but knowing about something and *not* acting upon it makes it a terrible waste. Now that you know how expensive debt is, *you owe it to yourself and to your loved ones to do something about it.*

I CHALLENGE YOU TO BE DIFFERENT

Being handcuffed by your mortgage doesn't have to be your way of life. Choose a different pathway to pay off your mortgage as described in this book, and it will pave the way to make your financial future brighter and sunnier.

You owe it to yourself and to your family.

Stay in touch, load your free spreadsheet, crunch your numbers, and be on your way to be mortgage free as quickly as you can.

WHAT ARE THE NEXT STEPS?

1. Download our free Excel mortgage amortization spreadsheet at www.financial-wisdom.net
2. If you feel a bit overwhelmed, go back and reread this book. You will be able to get more of the details and organize your thoughts and affairs better.
3. If you enjoy reading this book, it would be awesome if you could leave a quick review on Amazon on this link: www.amazon.com/1234567.

It only takes a minute, and it would be *greatly appreciated*. ☺ You can also share this book on Goodreads if that's one of your hangouts.

Wishing you all the very best!

Eric Blankenstein

January 2019

REFERENCES

1. https://www.consumerfinance.gov/data-research/consumer-credit-trends/mortgages/origination-activity
2. https://www.federalreserve.gov/data/mortoutstand/current.htm
3. Mortgage Daily. 2017. "Mortgage Daily 2016 Biggest Lender Ranking" [Press Release] Retrieved from https://globenewswire.com/news-release/2017/04/03/953457/0/en/Mortgage-Daily-2016-Biggest-Lender-Ranking.html.
4. https://www.bankofcanada.ca/wp-content/uploads/2013/12/fsr-december13-crawford.pdf
5. https://en.wikipedia.org/wiki/Home_equity
6. https://en.wikipedia.org/wiki/Mortgage_loan
7. https://smartasset.com/mortgage/what-is-the-typical-down-payment-on-a-home-purchase
8. https://www.fhfa.gov/Media/PublicAffairs/Pages/FHFA-Index-Shows-Mortgage-Rates-Increased-in-April-2018.aspx
9. https://www.thebalance.com/average-monthly-mortgage-payment-4154282
10. https://en.wikipedia.org/wiki/Home_equity_line_of_credit

11. https://www.irs.gov/newsroom/interest-on-home-equity-loans-often-still-deductible-under-new-law
12. http://www.moneychimp.com/features/market_cagr.htm
13. https://www.investopedia.com/investing/top-sp-500-etfs/
14. https://www.onepixel.com/search?search=mortgage
15. images courtesy of   https://pixy.org/

www.ingramcontent.com/pod-product-compliance
Lightning Source LLC
Chambersburg PA
CBHW021847170526
45157CB00007B/2981